OVERLOAD

BITE SIZED BIBLE STUDIES

Grace For The Pace

God's Word For
Stressed & Overloaded Lives

6 SESSIONS

BETH JONES

When your words came, I ate them;
they were my joy and my heart's delight . . .
Jeremiah 15:16 NIV

The Bite Sized Bible Study Series Includes . . .

- Satisfied Lives For Desperate Housewives: God's Word On Proverbs 31
- Kissed or Dissed: God's Word For Feeling Rejected & Overlooked
- Grace For The Pace: God's Word For Stressed & Overloaded Lives
- Don't Factor Fear Here: God's Word For Overcoming Anxiety, Fear & Phobias
- The Friends God Sends: God's Word On Friendship & Chick Chat
- What To Do When You Feel Blue: God's Word For Depression & Discouragement

Beth Jones is a Bible teacher, author, wife and mother of four children who ministers the Word of God in a relevant and inspiring way by sharing down-to-earth insights. She is the author of the popular Bible study series *Getting A Grip On The Basics* which is being used by thousands of churches in America and abroad, *Why The Gory, Bloody Details?*, and the *Bite Sized Bible Study Series*. Beth also writes a bi-weekly newspaper column titled *"Just Us Girls"* and hosts www.bethjones.org. She and her husband Jeff founded and serve as the senior pastors of Kalamazoo Valley Family Church.

Beth Jones may be reached @
Kalamazoo Valley Family Church, 269.324.5599
www.bethjones.org or www.kvfc.org

BITE SIZED BIBLE STUDIES

Grace For The Pace

God's Word For
Stressed & Overloaded Lives

6 SESSIONS

BETH JONES

Valley Press Publishers

Portage, MI

valleypresspublishers.com

Grace For The Pace
God's Word For Stressed & Overloaded Lives
ISBN: 1-933433-02-7
ISBN: 978-1933433-02-8

Published by Valley Press Publishers - A Ministry of KVFC
995 Romence Road, Portage, MI 49024
800-596-0379   www.kvfc.org

Contents

Acknowledgments

Writing a book is like having a baby! I've been "pregnant" with many books over the years and have found that once a book is "conceived" by the Holy Spirit and begins to grow, the gestation period can range from a few years to several decades. Then it seems that at the right time, when I'm "full-term" and "great with child", the Lord puts an "urge" to write within me which eventually triggers the labor pains, transition and ultimately the birth of a book! It takes a lot of people to give birth to a book and I'd like to honor those the Lord has put in my life to coach, pray, support and encourage me in these writing endeavors.

First, my husband, Jeff. You have been my best friend and most consistent encourager. When I have been uncertain, you've always been rock solid and gone the extra mile to help me fulfill God's will in writing. Thanks for loving me and believing in God's call on my life.

Second, my children, Meghan, Annie, Luke and Eric. I've had to take more time away to write; thanks for being understanding and willing to let mom go. I couldn't have asked for four better children. I love you all.

Third, my mom. What an inspiration you have always been to me! Thanks for letting me hang out with you in Florida to write these books.

Fourth, our staff. Our Associate Publisher, April Wedel, our Editorial Coordinator, Juli DeGraaf and our Publications Coordinator, Joanne Davis. I appreciate your love, faith, heart to get the Word out and the long hours you have spent helping me give birth to this book! I also want to thank the entire KVFC staff for their love, support and encouragement.

Fifth, all the volunteer copy editors and pray-ers. A very special thanks to Shannon Moldovan, Molly Nicolai and Dave Pinho for your time, comments and editing help. I especially appreciate my dear praying friends Mary VanderWal, Mary Jo Fox, Kate Cook, Cindy Boester, Jennifer Nederhoed, Pam Roe-Vanderberg, Jennifer Palthe, Colleen DeBruin, Molly Nicolai, KVFC prayer teams and many others who have continually lifted me and these projects to the Lord in prayer.

Sixth, Pat Judd, Bryan Norris and all the guys with CrossStaff. Thanks for partnering with us in this project. Let's have fun watching what the Lord will do!

The Heart
Of The
Bite Sized
Bible Studies

I love God's Word. I don't just like it; I love it. It's more valuable to me than anything. If I had to spend the rest of my life on a remote, uninhabited island and could only take one thing, I would take my Bible. Why? It's simple. God has changed and upgraded every area of my life as I have simply read, believed and obeyed the Bible.

It wasn't always that way. Like many people, I had never even considered reading the Bible for myself, much less studying it. The Bible was for priests, theologians and monks. It was not relevant to my life. It was a dusty old book in our basement. One day, when I was about 14 years old, I just got the "urge" to read the Bible. I started with Genesis, and within the first few chapters I fell asleep. That was the end of my Bible reading.

It wasn't until five years later when I was a 19-year-old college freshman that my roommate began to share with me what the Bible said about God, about life and about me. I was shocked at the "living" quality of the Bible. It wasn't like any other book I read. This wasn't like reading the president's biography. This wasn't like reading the dull Western Civilization textbooks in front of me. It was as if God Himself was explaining the contents to me. Something was happening in my heart as I read God's Word. I was challenged. I was encouraged. I was comforted. The Living God was speaking through His Living Word. During this time I developed a hunger for God and His Word. I stayed up late to read the Bible. I pondered it during the day. There was plenty I didn't understand, but I received strength, energy and wisdom just by reading it, and ultimately the Holy Spirit drew me to Jesus.

As a new Christian in my sophomore year of college, my Bible study leader simply exhorted me to read my Bible a lot and "let the Word of Christ dwell richly inside of me." It was the best advice ever! The result was that I began to develop an insatiable appetite for God's Word and a passionate desire to share God's Word with others. As I read my Bible, Jesus walked off the pages and came to live in my heart. Jesus isn't just alive in heaven, He is alive to me. I've come to know Him intimately through fellowship with Him in His Word.

Isn't it great that God's Word is interactive—not just historic or static? God's Word is living and active and able to effectually work within us to affect change and impart the miraculous! The Bible is the most amazing book ever! It has been banned, burned and blasted, but it lives on and continues to be the world's best-selling book.

Unfortunately, I have found that lots of people just don't understand the Bible and as a result, they get overwhelmed, bored or frustrated. Many Christians have never really tasted the rich, daily, life-changing flavor of God's Word. If you want to grow and mature in God, you have to "eat" large quantities of the Word. Once you taste and see that the Lord and His Word are good, nothing else will satisfy you! Think of it this way: if all you've ever tasted are peanut butter and jelly sandwiches, then you are pretty content with a good PBJ. But the minute you taste a filet mignon, you can never again be satisfied by a PBJ. In some ways, I have found that is the story for many Christians. If you're one of those people that have been content with a spiritual PBJ, I've got good news for you; get your taste buds ready for some rich, tasty, "meaty" morsels from God's Word. The more you eat it, the better it tastes!

Our goal in the Bite Sized Bible Study Series is to create an addiction in you for Bible study, and more importantly for knowing God intimately through the revelation knowledge of His Word, by His Spirit. As you explore these studies, I believe that the Holy Spirit will speak to your heart and transmit the supernatural revelation you need to operate victoriously in this life.

Jeremiah was right:

"When your words came, I ate them;
they were my joy and my heart's delight . . ."
Jeremiah 15:16, NIV

May this be your testimony, too!

How To Use This Bite Sized Bible Study

This Bible study can be used individually as well as in small groups. It's ideal for those who are hungry to learn from the Word, but who have a limited amount of time to meet together with others.

The Bite Sized Bible Study Series is designed for all types of Bible study formats.

- Individual Study
- Women's Small Groups
- Lunchtime Study at Work
- Neighborhood Bible Study
- Couples Small Groups
- Sunday School Class
- Prison Ministry
- Student and Youth Small Groups
- Outreach Bible Study
- Men's Bible Groups
- Singles Small Groups
- Recovery and Felt Need Groups

For Individual Study

Pray. Ask God, by the Holy Spirit, to customize these sessions for you personally.

Expect. Turn your "expectation" on and trust God to speak to your heart.

Dive. Grab your Bible, pen and favorite beverage and dive in!

For Small Group Study Leaders

Pray. Ask God, by the Holy Spirit, to reveal and customize these sessions for you and your group members.

Expect. Turn your "expectation" on and trust God to speak to your heart, as well as the hearts of those in your small group.

Facilitate. Small groups will do better with a facilitator, preferably a more mature Christian who can add helpful comments as well as lead a heartfelt time of prayer before and after each session. It's important that you keep things moving in the right direction. As the leader of the small group, keep in mind that it's your job to facilitate discussion and not act as the "teacher" who does all the talking. It's important for those in the group to verbalize their discoveries, so do your best to create an atmosphere where each member feels free to share what they are learning from God's Word.

Encourage. Encourage everyone to participate. Help those who talk a lot to take a breather and let others share their insights as well.

Focus. Stay focused on God the Father, Jesus, and the Holy Spirit Who gave us the Scriptures. Our goal is to see what God has said in His Word. Keep in mind that this is a Bible study and not a place for "my opinion" or "my church believes" or "here's what I think" comments. Always direct people's attention back to the Bible to see what the Scriptures say.

Highlight. Hit the high points. If you face time constraints, you may not have enough time to cover every detail of each lesson. As the leader, prayerfully prepare and be sure you cover the highlights of each session.

Digest. We've endeavored to "cut up" the Word through this Bite Sized Bible Study, and as a leader it's your job to help those in your small group digest the Scriptures so they can benefit from all the spiritual nutrition in each word.

Discuss. Take time to answer the three discussion questions at the end of each Bible study session. These should help stimulate heartfelt conversation.

First Things First

I f you want this Bible study to really impact your life, you must be certain of one major thing: you must be certain you are a Christian according to God's definition and instruction in the Bible. You must be certain that you are accepted by God; that you are saved. So let's begin our study by considering this important issue.

Did you know that some people want to be a Christian on their terms, rather than on God's terms? Sometimes people want to emphasize church, religion and their goodness as evidence of their Christianity. For some, it will be a rude awakening to discover that the Bible tells us God isn't impressed by any of those substitutes. Did you know that God isn't interested in our denominational tags? He's not wowed by our church membership pedigree, either. He's not moved by our good deeds and benevolent accomplishments. The thing that most impresses God is His Son, Jesus Christ. *"For God so loved the world that he gave his one and only Son, that whoever believes in him shall not perish but have eternal life."* *John 3:16, NIV* God paid quite a price to send His own Son to the cross to pay the penalty for our sin. It's really an insult to Him to trust in or substitute anything or anyone else for Jesus Christ. The key to being a Christian is to believe in, trust, receive and confess Jesus Christ as your Lord and Savior.

Why would you or anyone want to believe in, trust, receive and confess Jesus Christ as Lord? Why would you want to know Jesus personally and to be known by Him? Unless you truly understand your condition before God, you wouldn't have any reason to! However, when you realize the magnitude of your sin—those private and public thoughts, deeds, actions and words that you and God know about—when you listen to your conscience and realize that truly "all have sinned," including you, it can be very sobering. It's even more sobering to realize that according to God's justice system, *". . . the wages of sin is death . . ."* *Romans 6:23 NKJV* It's a big wake up call when it really hits you that the consequence of sin is death. Death which is defined as an eternal separation from God is the payment you will receive for your sin. When you realize your true, hopeless, lost condition before God, you will run to Him in order to be saved. This reality causes people to quit playing religious games and to quit trusting in their own works of righteousness. Our lost condition forces us to forgo being "churchy" or "religious", apathetic, passive and indifferent, and to become hungry for the Merciful Living God. It's good news to discover that " . . . *the gift of God is eternal life in Christ Jesus our Lord." Romans 6:23 NKJV*

What does God require of us? The qualification for eternal life is simply to believe on Jesus. Many people say they believe in God or in Jesus Christ. In fact, the Bible tells us that the devil himself believes and trembles. According to the Bible, God's definition of a Christian believer—or a Christ One—is the person who believes in their heart that God raised Jesus from the dead and who confesses with his or her mouth that Jesus Christ is their Lord. In other words, their heart and mouth agree that Jesus is Lord! We see this in Romans 10:13, 9, *". . . whoever calls on the name of the LORD shall be saved . . . if you confess with your mouth the Lord Jesus and believe in your heart that God has raised Him from the dead, you will be saved." NKJV*

This is something we do on purpose. It's a sobering thought to consider that if you've never purposely repented of your sin and invited Jesus Christ to be the Lord of your life, you may not be saved—you may not be a Christian according to God's definition. Would you like to be certain that you are a Christian; that you have a relationship with the Lord and eternal salvation? It's simple, just answer these questions: Do you believe that God raised Jesus from the dead? Will you give Him the steering wheel of your life and trust Him to forgive all your sins and make you an entirely new person? Will you trust Jesus Christ alone to save you? Are you willing to invite Him into your life and will you confess that He is your Lord? If so, please pray this prayer from your heart. God will hear you, Jesus Christ will forgive your sins and enter your life. You will be a Christian.

"Dear God, I come to you as a person who recognizes my condition before you. I see that I am a sinner in need of a Savior. Jesus, I do believe that God raised You from the dead and I now invite you into my life. I confess Jesus as my Lord. I want to know You and be the Christian You have called me to be, according to Your definition. I thank You, in Jesus' Name. Amen."

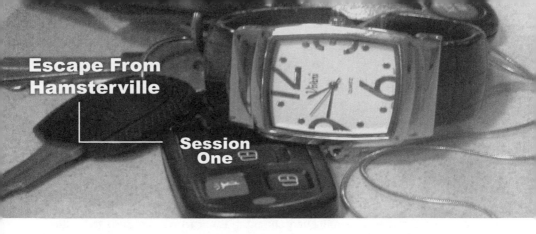

O verloaded. Stressed. Pressurized. Over-paced. Life is busy. I don't need to tell you that; you are likely living the life. Ever felt like the little hamster on the treadmill of life?

We were building a church and raising four elementary-aged kids. I was overloaded and feeling the stress. Like many people, we were living a very busy life. The candle was burning at both ends and we were pedaling as fast as we could to keep pace with our season of life. I needed help! There were numerous mornings that I awoke and as my feet hit the floor all I could say was, *"Grace, grace, God's grace, Grace that is greater than all my fears. Lord, I thank You for Grace."* I literally lived by those words. Through making that simple, heartfelt declaration of faith, I believe I accessed God's grace to help me with the pace of that season.

God understands the times we live in. Jesus knew that many people would be tempted to live life like the little hamster on the spinning wheel required to keep pace. The question is, how do you spin all the plates? How do you juggle every ball thrown at you? Let's visit Hamsterville.

Mr. and Mrs. Hamster are burning the candle at both ends trying to please one another, their kids, their boss, and their employees, while also being Super Hamsters. As soon as their feet hit the ground each day, they find themselves up on the spinning wheel and round and round they go, faster and faster. Daddy Hamster's day begins before the crack of dawn. He showers, shaves, gulps down a doubleshot espresso Hammucinno, and off to work he goes. He works hard all day; meeting with mice, guinea

When 100+ CEOs from top companies from around the world are on the wait list, that is 'stress!'

Wolfgang Hultner, General Manager Mandarin Oriental Hotel, San Francisco

pigs and gerbils, planning, making decisions, solving problems and desperately seeking to make a profit. He pushes his body to the limit . . . spinning the wheel, faster, faster and faster. By five o'clock he's beat. As he heads home to see Momma Ham and the little Hammies, he dreams about resting on his Aspen shavings while his little ones bring him his favorite plant roots. Unfortunately, when he arrives home he finds Mrs. Hamster and the little Hammies also had a busy day and they need his full, energetic attention. From dinnertime to bedtime he's on full-time "daddy duty." Just before bed, he checks his email and finally relaxes as he flips through the TV channels to watch another episode of Hamster Idol. What a day, and just think: he gets to do this again tomorrow! Sound familiar?

For Momma Ham, it's a busy life. She wakes up early to the pitter-patter of Hammie paws. She sets out the seeds and tells the Hammies to quit chewing on the cage. Her chauffeuring duties begin as she hops into her SUV, Hammer2, and drops off her little ones at school while making sure her oldest drives to Hamster High safely. She stops by the salon to get her Hamicure and when she arrives back to the cage she spends the rest of the day cleaning up droppings, washing the wheel and using her mental, emotional and physical energy spinning on the wheel. By six o'clock, everyone is back home and the night schedule kicks in. Momma Ham helps the kids with Hamework while dad takes the other Hammies to wheel-spinning practice. By midnight, Mr. and Mrs. Hamster are ready to collapse on the couch!

Have you lived this life? Keeping up with the Hamsters leads to mental and emotional burn out! Life these days is busy. Is it possible to work, maintain a home and raise a family without burning out? Can parents keep up? Unfortunately, many people are pressured to operate with zero margin— emotionally, physically, financially, spiritually. It's taking a toll. The emotional quotient that is required for daily living—financial pressures, caring for aging parents, protecting our kids, watching out for terrorists and the list goes on—is a major drain on our lives. Then . . . add the need to keep up technologically. The Internet, as wonderful as it is, has opened up an entirely new set of pressures "to know." Information overload is draining. Technology is changing at such a rapid rate it takes 3 weeks just to research which TV to buy. That's stress!

For Christians, there is an added degree of stress and pressure. Believers are expected to be Christ-like at all times, to love their enemies and volunteer for charitable service, while at the same time rejoicing as they are being persecuted, mocked, laughed at or criticized for their faith in Jesus Christ. It can be overwhelming.

You get the picture. Psychologists and researchers could tell you more. I've discovered that without recognizing God's "grace for the pace," it is impossible to keep up in this stressed and overloaded life. So, as we launch into this study, let's define grace.

&**Nugget**&   What is "grace for the pace"? What does it look like? There are many definitions for grace. Many times it's described as something spiritually ethereal, but grace is not a theory; it's tangible! Grace is a tangible, spiritual commodity. God in His goodness gives us grace deposits!

Grace: Grace is from the Greek word "charis" and there are many definitions for this rich word. Perhaps you've heard the grace acrostic: "God's Riches At Christ's Expense." According to Greek scholars, the word grace has meanings which include the divine influence upon the heart, and its reflection in the life; including gratitude. This word is also translated as the word benefit, gift and favor.[1]

Grace is also seen as that kindness by which God bestows favors even upon the ill-deserving, and grants to sinners the pardon of their offences, and bids them to accept eternal salvation through Christ. Grace is used of the merciful kindness by which God, exerting His holy influence upon souls, turns them to Christ, keeps, strengthens, increases them in Christian faith, knowledge, affection, and kindles them to the exercise of the Christian virtues.[2]

God's grace is manifold. The Bible describes at least three different categories of grace: saving grace, standing grace and serving grace.

Saving grace is the grace God gives to sinners to influence their hearts and turn them to Christ. We cannot be saved apart from God's grace. According to Ephesians 2:8-9, *"For it is by grace you have been saved, through faith - and* this not from yourselves, it is the gift of God - not by works, so that no one can boast." *NIV* Think about your own salvation. Do you remember how God graced you in such a way that you were able to have faith to believe? God's saving grace allows us to have faith to believe and be saved. It's truly a gift!

Standing grace is the grace God gives us to stand in faith and live the Christian life. We need God's grace to live! Romans 5:1-2 tells us, *"Therefore, since we have been justified through faith, we have peace with God through our Lord Jesus Christ, through whom we have gained access by faith into this grace in which we now stand." NIV* Through faith we stand in grace. God's grace gives us the ability to have faith, to know, to grow, to think, to give, to be and to do all the things God wants for us. I would venture to say that most believers are unfamiliar with "standing grace," but it is this very grace that we are talking about when we seek the Lord for "grace for the pace." When God gives us standing grace He gives us His ability for various areas of our lives. As Keith Green once sang in his song *Grace By Which I Stand, "Nothing lasts except the grace of God by which I stand."*

Serving grace is the grace God gives us to serve Him. He gives us grace gifts, talents, passions and callings that are unique to each one of us. God has graced or gifted each of us in a special way so that we can serve Him in a powerful and fruitful manner. Whether your serving grace is in the area of leadership, hospitality, teaching, mercy, giving or some other area, God enables and equips you for serving by His grace. The Apostle Paul understood serving grace when he said, *"We have different gifts, according to the grace given us." Romans 12:6, NIV* He also said, *"But by the grace of God I am what I am, and his grace to me was not without effect. No, I worked harder than all of them-yet not I, but the grace of God that was with me." 1 Corinthians 15:10, NIV* Notice that Paul said that it was the grace of God within him that allowed him to work and serve God. Each one of us has been endowed with serving grace that also helps us function in the "grace for the pace."

I believe that one of the most powerful promises in the Bible is Romans 5:17: *"For if, by the trespass of the one man, death reigned through that one man, how much more will those who receive God's abundant provision of grace and of the gift of righteousness reign in life through the one man, Jesus Christ." NIV*

When we truly receive God's abundant provision of grace—saving grace, standing grace and serving grace—and His gift of righteousness, we can reign in life. What would it mean to you if you were to reign in life? It means that we learn how to overcome every bit of stress and overload that is thrown our way. I encourage you to open your heart as we study the power of God's grace for the pace.

⧫**Nugget**⧫   Simply put: *Grace for the pace is when God Almighty gives us a supernatural deposit or endowment of inner strength, giftings, ability, know-how, understanding, knowledge and favor which first leads us to salvation, and which helps us stand in victory and serve God.* God's grace helps us with the pace—the stressed and overloaded lives we often face. We need God's grace for the pace! Grace is His free gift to man. It's the most amazing thing, that God Almighty would impart His grace to us and that grace would supernaturally help us succeed in whatever we face! When we truly receive God's grace for the pace, we receive the ability to function at the pace required of us. Living in the grace is to receive, recognize and identify our God-given gifts and bents, and connect them with the God-given season and callings in our lives. Like a glove and hand, God's grace and our life work together in a supernatural rhythm. In practical terms, grace for the pace is when God graces us to be a Christian, a wife, a husband, a mom, a dad, a friend, a businessperson, an entrepreneur, an athlete, a builder, engineer, doctor, lawyer, homemaker, manager, chef, clerk, pastor, evangelist, coach, volunteer, banker, baker, candlestick maker and the list goes on. If you have grace . . . life is like a well-greased machine. There's a flow. There's supernatural ease. You know when to say yes and when to say no. Whatever you need to know, be or do—God wants to grace you in such a way that you have His supernatural ability in that area. Grace is huge! Can you see how wonderful God's grace is?

⧫**Nugget**⧫   The other side of the coin is this: without grace you will eventually burn out and resent the very things you once loved. Without grace you'll do what you have to do, but eventually you'll start to feel like a

It's not stress that kills us, it is our reaction to it.

Hans Selye
Stress Expert

"flat-liner" in life, and you will experience a sense of detachment. Without grace you function, but there's no unction. You survive, but you do not thrive. You may be skilled, but you are not fulfilled. You live and die, but never know why. Get the picture? Without God's grace for the pace, in the end there will be sorrow and regret.

Now, let's dive into God's Word to see what He has to say about stress and overloaded lives.

The Need For Speed

1.   John 16:33

Underline the phrase "in Me you may have peace."

These things I have spoken to you, that in Me you may have peace. In the world you will have tribulation; but be of good cheer, I have overcome the world. NKJV

What did Jesus promise we would have in this world? _____

Jesus said we would face stress and overload in this life. The word "tribulation" comes from the Greek word "thlipsis," which literally and figuratively means "pressure." It's also translated as: anguish, burden, trouble, persecution.[3] In other words, stress and overload!

Describe a time you felt anguished or burdened or troubled or persecuted or pressured.

_____

What did Jesus tell us to do in response to pressure? _____

_____

What does Jesus promise us in Him? _____

_____

2.   Proverbs 24:10

Underline the word that describes stress.

If you fail under pressure, your strength is not very great. NLT

What is the purpose of pressure, busyness and stress?

_____

If we cave into pressure, what does this tell us about ourselves?

_____

Nugget   This is a wake-up call. The enemy's goal is that we are so busy, pressured, stressed and overwhelmed that we lose touch with God and our vital personal relationship with Him, and that we fail in life's endeavors. It's important that we are strong in the Lord and continually strengthening our inner man so that our emotional, mental and physical life is energized, enabling us to overcome in life.

3.   Luke 10:38-42

Underline the phrases "Martha [overly occupied and too busy] was distracted" and "Martha, Martha, you are anxious and troubled about many things."

38 Now while they were on their way, it occurred that Jesus entered a certain village, and a woman named Martha received and welcomed Him into her house. 39 And she had a sister named Mary, who seated herself at the Lord's feet and was listening to His teaching. 40 But Martha [overly occupied and too busy] was distracted with much serving; and she came up to Him and said, Lord, is it nothing to You that my sister has left me to serve alone? Tell her then to help me [to lend a hand and do her part along with me]! 41 But the Lord replied to her by saying, Martha, Martha, you are anxious and troubled about many things; 42 There is need of only one or but a few things. Mary has chosen the good portion [that which is to her advantage], which shall not be taken away from her. AMP

This is such a great story because we can all relate to it. We all want to be Mary, but many of us are Martha.

What type of person was Martha? _____

What type of person was Mary? _____

Do you know some Marthas and Marys? _____

Which one are you? _____

What was Martha's priority? _____

What was Mary's priority? _____

Who had more stress? _____

Why was Martha so stressed out? _____

We often live like Martha at work, at home and in ministry. Jesus loved Martha, but He had to set her straight. Jesus clarified the difference between "many things" and "one thing."

What are the "many things" that distract and pressure you?_____

_____

What is the "one thing" Jesus said was needed? _____

_____

What do you think the phrase "one thing is needed" means? _____

_____

The biggest secret of this story is found in verse 42.

What did Mary do? _____

Describe the challenge of "choosing" in your own life.

_____

_____

≈**Nugget**≈   I think Martha may have been a Type A personality.
Maybe you're a Type A personality. You've heard
the term, right? How do you know if you're a Type
A? According to psychologist Shelly Wu, Ph.D,
these traits fit the Type A personality.[4]

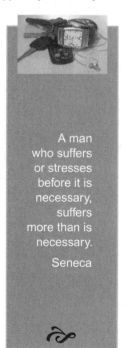

1. Type A people are always on the move.

2. Type A people have a strong sense of urgency.

3. Type A people often sit at the edge of their
    seats, literally.

4. Type A people check their watches more
    frequently.

5. Type A people are often obsessed with their
    work.

A man
who suffers
or stresses
before it is
necessary,
suffers
more than is
necessary.

Seneca

≈

6. Type A people are extremely competitive.

7. Type A people want to get things done and they will do almost anything to accomplish their goals.

8. Type A people tend to become aggressive, impatient, and irritable at anyone or anything that interferes with their work.

9. Type A people are more likely to get heart disease.

10. Once they have the disease, they are more likely to diligently follow their doctors' orders. Therefore, they are also more likely to recover from the disease.

Does this describe you? _____

4.   James 1:10

Underline the last sentence.

But a rich man should be glad that his riches mean nothing to the Lord, for he will soon be gone, like a flower that has lost its beauty and fades away, withered-killed by the scorching summer sun. So it is with rich men. They will soon die and leave behind all their busy activities. TLB

Putting things in perspective is always a good idea. What does this verse tell us about the end result of all our busy pursuits?

_____

_____

Jesus said, *"For what will it profit a man if he gains the whole world, and loses his own soul?" Mark 8:36 NKJV* If busyness, pressures, stress and overload cause us to lose perspective and misplace our priorities, we are missing it.

᭞**Nugget**᭞ We've known person after person and family after family that has become so busy in their own pursuits that seeking God and His Church gets squeezed right out of their lives. It's a formula for disaster. Perhaps you've noticed the same thing. When people put their job, soccer, football, basketball, travel, hobbies, sleep and personal projects in the slot reserved for God alone, they run the risk of facing personal, marital, business and health problems. We've seen it first hand. We've watched one family after another get busy with successful careers, educational pursuits, fitness goals and children's sporting or extracurricular activities. We've seen Jesus go to the back burner as church attendance became less and less frequent. Unfortunately, we've watched those same families experience marital, emotional, relational, financial and health-related problems that have taken a huge toll on their lives. It's not worth it. Jesus told us, *"But seek first the kingdom of God and His righteousness, and all these things shall be added to you."* *Matthew 6:33, NKJV* When we seek God first, He gives us the grace and blessings that go along with His kingdom. When we decide to run the show in our own energy and wisdom, then we are on our own and we face the toll that stress and overload takes on us and our families.

5.   2 Corinthians 4:8-9

Underline the words "hard pressed," "perplexed," "persecuted" and "struck down."

8 We are hard-pressed on every side, yet not crushed; we are perplexed, but not in despair; 9 persecuted, but not forsaken; struck down, but not destroyed... NKJV

This passage describes the "almost breaking" point of stress and pressure. What four words describe stress and pressure?

_____   _____

_____   _____

In what areas of your life do you feel these pressures? _____

_____

What four words describe our ability to stand strong?

_____   _____

_____   _____

6. Psalm 61:2

Underline the phrase "when my heart is overwhelmed."

From the end of the earth I will cry to You, when my heart is overwhelmed; lead me to the rock that is higher than I. NKJV

What do we do when we feel overwhelmed? _____

Who is the Rock? _____

If you are overwhelmed, run to the Rock! Jesus is the Rock and we can always run to Him. Perhaps you need to spend some time just getting quiet, praying, listening to worship music and reading your Bible. Let your heart settle in with Him.

Slow Down

Simon and Garfunkel sang the classic song, *"Feelin' Groovy"*, which still describes our times.

"Slow down, don't move too fast
You've got to make the morning last
Kickin' down the cobblestones
Lookin' for fun and feelin' groovy
Feelin' groovy . . ."

Do you remember that song? We live in the hurry up world. Doctors have even identified a "hurry up syndrome"!

The term *hurry sickness* was coined back in the 1950s when cardiologists Meyer Friedman and Ray Rosenman were researching personality types. By 1959 they had refined this to the now-classic *Type A personality*, a key element of which was a "harrying sense of time urgency."[5]

☙Nugget☙   In his book, *Faster: The Acceleration of Just About Everything*, James Gleick describes the fact that never in the history of the human race have so many had so much to do in so little time.[6] He says, *"Most of us suffer some degree of 'hurry sickness,' a malady that has launched us into the 'epoch of the nanosecond,' a need-everything-yesterday sphere dominated by cell phones, computers, faxes, and remote controls. Yet for all the hours, minutes, and even seconds being saved, we're still filling our days to the point that we have no time for such basic human activities as eating, sex, and relating to our families."*

The Hurried Woman Syndrome is affecting as many as 30 million women each year, according to Dr. Brent W. Bosts' book by the same title.[7] The Hurried Woman Syndrome can drain your energy, cause you to gain weight (or have trouble keeping your weight stable), increase your moodiness and frustration, and ultimately lower your sexual energy as well.

According to Dr. Bosts, the three major symptoms of the Hurried Woman Syndrome are:

- Fatigue or a low mood

- Weight gain

- Low sex drive (libido)

He goes on to say that, " . . . *women, usually between the ages of 25 and 55 and often with children between the ages of 4 and 16, are most often affected by the*

For fast-acting relief try slowing down.

Lily Tomlin

Hurried Woman Syndrome. Many Hurried Women work outside the home, but a large number of women who suffer with the syndrome stay at home. Even women who don't have children can come down with it—a stressful career, sick relative, or burdensome responsibilities can all contribute to making the symptoms worse. Stress is probably the single most important factor that causes women to complain about the Hurried Woman Syndrome. There are many types of stress and they vary from patient to patient. Sometimes the stress can't be avoided, such as a sick child or a high-powered career. However, for the majority of women, much of the stress is avoidable or at least could be managed better. These avoidable stresses are those that often come from a busy, hectic schedule and lifestyle choices that many of us have embraced as completely "normal." Yet, the effects of this kind of stress— what I call "hurry"—can have very significant long-term and wide-reaching consequences for the woman who labors under it and those around her who suffer along with her."

Does God have answers to the hurry up world we live in? Of course! We see in the Word that there are legitimate times to hurry; when God tells you to run, to escape danger, to tell the good news, etc. We also see that those who live by faith don't make haste; there is a degree of patience and the ability to wait on the Lord that is healthy and godly.

1.   Jeremiah 2:25

        Underline the reason people were in a hurry.

        Slow down. Take a deep breath. What's the hurry? Why wear yourself out? Just what are you after anyway? But you say, 'I can't help it. I'm addicted to alien gods. I can't quit.' The Message

        There are many "gods" pulling for our affection, time and attention.

        What are the alien gods in your life? _____

&**Nugget**& Unfortunately, in America one of the biggest alien gods that families worship is "sports"! Yup, basketball practice, hockey ice time, soccer tournaments and the like have invaded every day of the week, including Sunday mornings, and many parents are teaching their children how to worship athletics instead of Jesus Christ. I know it's a bitter pill to swallow, but it is the absolute truth in these days. Parents wear themselves out trying to get their children to practice and travel team games, secretly hoping that it produces a full ride college scholarship for their child at the expense of their spiritual life. I realize that occasional games or tournaments arise and sometimes those cannot be helped, but for many families it's not "occasional," it's "regular." When the kids hit the teen years, parents wonder, *"I don't know why my son or daughter just doesn't like church or youth group. They said it's not fun. I'm not going to make them go, it's their choice."* The reason they don't like church or youth group is because that's what you taught them! You helped them worship alien gods and now they don't have the desire to worship the Living God, unless it's "fun." Isn't that sad? It's true, nonetheless. Why do parents give their kids a "choice" when it comes to attending church and youth group, but they would never dream of giving that same child the "choice" of attending a sports practice or game? Alien gods.

Other alien gods include: golfing, gardening, sleeping, boating, skiing, the cottage . . . you get the idea? I know I am hitting close to home. Sure, God wants us to enjoy life and recreation, but not at His expense. If any "alien god" is taking His place, eating up His time and spending His money, then it's time to slow down and return to the King of kings and the Lord of lords.

2.   Isaiah 28:16

Underline the phrase "whoever believes will not act hastily."

Therefore thus says the Lord GOD: "Behold, I lay in Zion a stone for a foundation, a tried stone, a precious cornerstone, a sure foundation; whoever believes will not act hastily. NKJV

Jesus is the Precious Cornerstone and our Sure Foundation. This verse tells us that he who believes in Him as their sure foundation will not be given to do what?

_____

The idea is that there is a rest for the believer. They do not need to panic, hurry, be dismayed in any way, but their faith in Jesus Christ provides stability.

3.   Proverbs 28:20

Underline the results of being too hasty.

"A faithful man will abound with blessings, but he who hastens to be rich will not go unpunished." NKJV

What is this person hurrying to do? _____

What's the difference between a "faithful man" and one who "hastens to be rich"?

_____

What is the result of the person who hurries to be rich?

_____

There are some things we do need to be in a "hurry" to do. What are those things according to these verses?

- Psalm 119:60, _"I made haste, and did not delay to keep Your commandments." NKJV_

_____

- Luke 19:5, *"When Jesus got to the tree, he looked up and said, "Zacchaeus, hurry down. Today is my day to be a guest in your home." The Message*

- Isaiah 26:7-8, *"The path of right-living people is level. The Leveler evens the road for the right-living. We're in no hurry, GOD. We're content to linger in the path sign-posted with your decisions. Who you are and what you've done are all we'll ever want." The Message*

- Isaiah 40:28-31, *"28 Have you never heard or understood? Don't you know that the LORD is the everlasting God, the Creator of all the earth? He never grows faint or weary. No one can measure the depths of his understanding. 29 He gives power to those who are tired and worn out; he offers strength to the weak. 30 Even youths will become exhausted, and young men will give up. 31 But those who wait on the LORD will find new strength. They will fly high on wings like eagles. They will run and not grow weary. They will walk and not faint." NLT*

Satan's Meeting

This e-mail written by Charles A. Beard went around a few years ago, and unfortunately carries a degree of truth:

Satan called a world wide convention of demons. In his opening address he said "We can't keep Christians from going to church. We can't keep them from reading their bibles and knowing the truth. We can't even keep them from forming an intimate relationship with their Savior. Once they gain that connection with Jesus, our power over them is broken. So let them go to their churches. Let them have their covered dish dinners, BUT steal their time so they don't have time to develop a relationship with Jesus Christ. This is what I want you to do," said the devil. "Distract them from gaining hold of their Savior and maintaining that vital connection throughout their day!" "How shall we do this?" his demons shouted.

"Keep them busy in the nonessentials of life and invent innumerable schemes to occupy their minds," he answered. "Tempt them to spend, spend, spend and borrow, borrow, borrow. Persuade the wives to go to work for long hours and the husbands to work 6-7 days each week, 10-12 hrs a day, so they can afford their empty lifestyles. Keep them from spending time with their children. As their families begin to fragment, soon their homes will offer no escape from the pressures of work! Over stimulate their minds so they cannot hear that still small voice. Entice them to play the radio or cassette player whenever they drive, and to keep the TV, VCR, CD's, and their PC's going constantly in their home. See to it that every store and restaurant in the world plays non-biblical music constantly. This will jam their minds and break that union with Christ. Fill the coffee tables with magazines and newspapers. Pound their minds with the news 24 hours a day. Invade their driving moments with billboards, flood their mailboxes with junk mail and mail order catalogs, sweepstakes, and every kind of newsletter and promotional offering free products, services and false hopes. Keep skinny beautiful models on the magazines and TV so their husbands will believe that outward beauty is what's important, and they'll become dissatisfied with their wives.

Keep the wives too tired to love their husbands at night. Give them headaches, too! If they don't give their husbands the love they need, they will begin to look elsewhere. That will fragment their families quickly! Give them Santa Claus to distract them from teaching their children the real meaning of Christmas. Give them an Easter Bunny so they won't talk about His resurrection and power over sin and death. Even in their recreation, let them be excessive. Have them return from their recreation exhausted. Keep them too busy to go out in nature and reflect on God's creation.

Send them to amusement parks, sporting events, plays, concerts, and movies instead. Keep them busy, busy, busy! And when they meet for spiritual *fellowship, involve them in gossip and small talk so that they leave with troubled consciences. Crowd their lives with so many good causes, they have no time to seek power from Jesus. Soon they will be working on their own strength, sacrificing their health and family for the good of the cause. It will work! It will work!"*

It was quite a plan! The demons went eagerly to their assignments causing Christians everywhere to get more busy and more rushed, going here and there, having little time for God and their families, having no time to tell others about the power of Jesus to change lives. I guess the question is, has the devil been successful at his scheme? You be the judge! Does "busy" mean: B-eing, U-nder, S-atans, Y-oke?

God has a better plan! If you've felt like the busy, stressed-out and overloaded hamster on the treadmill, it's time to enter into God's rest and tap into His grace for the pace. Hebrew 4:3 says, *"For we which have believed do enter into rest . . ."* KJV

Scriptures To Chew On

Taking time to meditate on and memorize God's Word is invaluable. Hiding His Word in our hearts will strengthen us for the present and arm us for the future. Here are two verses to memorize and chew on this week. Write these verses on index cards and carry them with you this week. If you will post them in your bathroom, dashboard, desk, locker or other convenient places, you will find these Scriptures taking root in your heart.

*"Be still, and know that I am God:
I will be exalted among the heathen,
I will be exalted in the earth."
Psalm 46:10, KJV*

*"For we which have believed do enter into rest . . ."
Hebrews 4:3, KJV*

Group Discussion

1.   Describe the pace of your own life. What plates are you required to spin and how many balls do you have to juggle?

2.   Describe your experience with God's saving grace. How did you come to Christ?

3.   Describe the things that tempt and distract you to lose the focus of your priorities. In your experience, what "alien gods" do you and those in our society struggle with?

[1]Biblesoft's New Exhaustive Strong's Numbers and Concordance with Expanded Greek-Hebrew Dictionary. Copyright © 1994, 2003 Biblesoft, Inc. and International Bible Translators, Inc.

[2]Thayer's Greek Lexicon, Electronic Database. Copyright (c) 2000 by Biblesoft

[3]Biblesoft, as above.

[4]About.com (http://psychology.about.com/library/howto/httypea.htm)

[5] http://www.wordspy.com/words/hurrysickness.asp

[6] Gleik, James. Faster: The Acceleration of Just About Everything. New York: Pantheon Books, 1999.

[7] Bost, Brent W. The Hurried Woman Syndrome. New York: McGraw-Hill, 2005.

Personal Notes

Personal Notes

God never intended for us to live life without help. We need Him. We need His grace. Our good friend, Tony Cooke, posts the story of the bricklayer on his website (www.tonycooke.org) which paints the picture—we need help!

Trying To Do The Job Alone

Dear Sir:

I am writing in response to your request for additional information for my insurance claim. In block number three of the accident claim form I wrote, "trying to do the job alone" as the cause of my accident. You said in your letter that I should explain that statement more fully. I trust the following details will be sufficient.

I am a bricklayer by trade. On the date of the accident, I was working alone on the roof of a new six-story building. When I completed my work I discovered that I had about 500 pounds of brick left over. Rather than carrying the bricks down by hand, I decided to lower them in a barrel by using a pulley which was attached to the side of the building at the sixth-floor level.

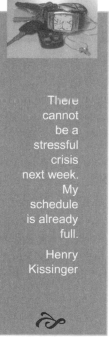

There cannot be a stressful crisis next week. My schedule is already full.

Henry Kissinger

Securing the rope at ground level, I went up to the roof, swung the barrel out, and loaded the bricks into it. Then I went back to the ground and untied the rope, holding it tightly to insure a slow descent of the 500 pounds of bricks. You will note in block number 22 of the claim form that my weight is 150 pounds.

Due to my surprise at being jerked off the ground so suddenly, I lost my
presence of mind and forgot to let go of the rope. Needless to say, I proceeded
up the side of the building at a very rapid rate of speed. In the vicinity of the
third floor, I met the barrel coming down. This explains my fractured skull and
collarbone. Slowed only slightly, I continued my rapid ascent, not stopping
until the fingers of my right hand were two knuckles deep into the pulley.
By this time, I had regained my presence of mind and was able to hold tightly
to the rope in spite of my pain. At approximately the same time however, the
barrel of bricks hit the ground and the bottom fell out of the barrel. Devoid of
the weight of the bricks, the barrel then weighed approximately 50 pounds.
I refer you again to the information in block number 11 regarding my weight.
As you might imagine, I began a rapid descent down the side of the building. In
the vicinity of the third floor, I met the barrel coming up. This accounts for the
two fractured ankles and the lacerations of my legs and lower body.
This second encounter with the barrel slowed me enough to lessen my injuries
when I fell onto the pile of bricks, and fortunately, only three vertebrae were
cracked.

I am sorry to report, however, that as I lay there on the bricks in pain, unable
to stand, and watching the empty barrel six stories above me, I again lost my
presence of mind, and let go of the rope. The empty barrel weighed more than
the rope so it came down upon me and broke both of my legs.

I hope I have furnished information sufficient to explain why "trying to do the
job alone" was the stated cause of the accident.

Sincerely,

A Bricklayer
(Author Unknown)

&Nugget&   Trying to do the job alone is not God's plan! My husband and I
have learned this lesson in marriage and ministry. Together we are more effective
than either of us would be alone. We realize that God has "graced" us with His
saving, standing and serving grace to function as a team and help each other at
home and at work. When we operate in the awareness of this grace, although we

live busy lives with the potential for overload, we find there is a supernatural help, ease and ability to function. This grace helps us in such menial, non-stop things like household chores, laundry, cleaning, grocery shopping and chauffeuring kids all over town. There is grace to do it as a team. We've also learned that in some areas of operating our home, we've needed outside help. Rather than trying to do it all, we've hired people to help us with housework, yard work, etc. Sometimes you will find that just taking one item off your plate will give you a big sense of relief. If there's grace to do everything, do it. But if you sense the need to hire some outside help, believe God for the funds and do it!

At work, the ministry and needs of the congregation keep us pedaling as fast as we can. We operate as a husband/wife pastoral team and we've learned (sometimes by trial and error) to operate in roles where God's grace is evident. It takes honesty and humility. This approach works because we've learned that rather than letting our own ego and pride get in the way because one of us is graced in an area where the other is not, we encourage each other to exercise their specific grace. Make sense? God is the One doling out grace gifts, so it makes sense to flow with what He's ordered rather than swim upstream without the grace.

Let's get into God's Word to look at "grace to help."

God Gives You Grace To Help

1.   Hebrews 4:16

        Underline the words "throne of grace" and "find grace to help."

        Let us therefore come boldly to the throne of grace, that we may obtain mercy and find grace to help in time of need. NKJV

        What does God call His very throne? _____

        What can we obtain at God's throne? _____

The Amplified Bible details this: *Let us then fearlessly and confidently and boldly draw near to the throne of grace (the throne of God's unmerited favor to us sinners), that we may receive mercy [for our failures] and find grace to help in good time for every need [appropriate help and well-timed help, coming just when we need it]. Hebrews 4:16, AMP*

According to this verse, what will grace do for you? _____

Notice this "grace to help" is there for our time of need.

How should you approach God's throne in order to receive "grace to help"?

_____

Don't hesitate. Because of your relationship with Jesus Christ, you can approach God's throne of grace with boldness to receive His mercy and find grace to help you in every time of need, including times of stress, pressure and busyness.

Let's take a moment, right now to pray for grace. *"Father, I am so thankful that because of the blood of Jesus Christ, the saving grace you've given to me and my union with Him, I can come into Your Presence with boldness. You said I could obtain mercy and find grace to help at Your throne of grace and Father, I thank You for that. Right now, I appropriate your mercy and grace and I ask You to impart a fresh dose of Your standing and serving grace into my life to help me in every arena. I thank You, Lord, that right now I believe I receive a deposit of grace from Your very throne. Thank You. In Jesus' Name. Amen."*

2.   Acts 27:1-44

Underline the word "helps." This is a long passage, but one that describes in living color the reality of pressure and stress. The Apostle Paul was in the storm of his life. If you've ever felt your "boat" rocking in the storms created by an overwhelmed life, you'll appreciate this story and see a simple principle that helped Paul during this storm.

1 And when it was determined that we should sail into Italy, they delivered Paul and certain other prisoners unto one named Julius, a centurion of Augustus' band. 2 And entering into a ship of Adramyttium, we launched, meaning to sail by the coasts of Asia; one Aristarchus, a Macedonian of Thessalonica, being with us. 3 And the next day we touched at Sidon. And Julius courteously entreated Paul, and gave him liberty to go unto his friends to refresh himself. 4 And when we had launched from thence, we sailed under Cyprus, because the winds were contrary. 5 And when we had sailed over the sea of Cilicia and Pamphylia, we came to Myra, a city of Lycia. 6 And there the centurion found a ship of Alexandria sailing into Italy; and he put us therein. 7 And when we had sailed slowly many days, and scarce were come over against Cnidus, the wind not suffering us, we sailed under Crete, over against Salmone; 8 And, hardly passing it, came unto a place which is called The fair havens; nigh whereunto was the city of Lasea. 9 Now when much time was spent, and when sailing was now dangerous, because the fast was now already past, Paul admonished them, 10 And said unto them, Sirs, I perceive that this voyage will be with hurt and much damage, not only of the lading and ship, but also of our lives. 11 Nevertheless the centurion believed the master and the owner of the ship, more than those things which were spoken by Paul. 12 And because the haven was not commodious to winter in, the more part advised to depart thence also, if by any means they might attain to Phenice, and there to winter; which is an haven of Crete, and lieth toward the south west and north west. 13 And when the south wind blew softly, supposing that they had obtained their purpose, loosing thence, they sailed close by Crete. 14 But not long after there arose against it a tempestuous wind, called Euroclydon. 15 And when the ship was caught, and could not bear up into the wind, we let her drive. 16 And running under a certain island which is called Clauda, we had much

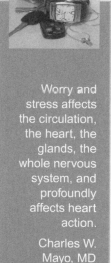

Worry and stress affects the circulation, the heart, the glands, the whole nervous system, and profoundly affects heart action.

Charles W. Mayo, MD

work to come by the boat: 17 Which when they had taken up, they used helps, undergirding the ship; and, fearing lest they should fall into the quicksands, strake sail, and so were driven. 18 And we being exceedingly tossed with a tempest, the next day they lightened the ship; 19 And the third day we cast out with our own hands the tackling of the ship. 20 And when neither sun nor stars in many days appeared, and no small tempest lay on us, all hope that we should be saved was then taken away. 21 But after long abstinence Paul stood forth in the midst of them, and said, Sirs, ye should have hearkened unto me, and not have loosed from Crete, and to have gained this harm and loss. 22 And now I exhort you to be of good cheer: for there shall be no loss of any man's life among you, but of the ship. 23 For there stood by me this night the angel of God, whose I am, and whom I serve, 24 Saying, Fear not, Paul; thou must be brought before Caesar: and, lo, God hath given thee all them that sail with thee. 25 Wherefore, sirs, be of good cheer: for I believe God, that it shall be even as it was told me. 26 Howbeit we must be cast upon a certain island. 27 But when the fourteenth night was come, as we were driven up and down in Adria, about midnight the shipmen deemed that they drew near to some country; 28 And sounded, and found it twenty fathoms: and when they had gone a little further, they sounded again, and found it fifteen fathoms. 29 Then fearing lest we should have fallen upon rocks, they cast four anchors out of the stern, and wished for the day. 30 And as the shipmen were about to flee out of the ship, when they had let down the boat into the sea, under colour as though they would have cast anchors out of the foreship, 31 Paul said to the centurion and to the soldiers, Except these abide in the ship, ye cannot be saved. 32 Then the soldiers cut off the ropes of the boat, and let her fall off. 33 And while the day was coming on, Paul besought them all to take meat, saying, This day is the fourteenth day that ye have tarried and continued fasting, having taken nothing. 34 Wherefore I pray you to take some meat: for this is for your health: for there shall not an hair fall from the head of any of you. 35 And when he had thus spoken, he took bread, and gave thanks to God in presence of them all: and when he had broken it, he began to eat. 36 Then were they all of good cheer, and they also took some meat. 37 And we were in all in *the ship two hundred threescore and sixteen souls. 38 And when they had eaten enough, they lightened the ship, and cast out the wheat into the sea. 39 And when it was day, they knew not the land: but they discovered a certain creek with a shore, into the which they were minded, if it were possible, to thrust in the ship. 40 And when they had taken up the anchors, they committed themselves unto the sea, and loosed the rudder bands, and hoised up the mainsail to the wind, and made toward shore. 41 And falling into a place where two seas met, they ran the ship aground; and the forepart stuck fast, and remained unmoveable, but the hinder part was broken with the violence of the waves. 42 And the soldiers' counsel was to kill the prisoners, lest any of them should swim out, and escape. 43 But the centurion, willing to save Paul, kept them from their purpose; and commanded that they which could swim should cast themselves first into the sea, and get to land: 44 And the rest, some on boards, and some on broken pieces of the ship. And so it came to pass, that they escaped all safe to land. KJV*

Verse 10: What did Paul perceive about his journey? _____

Verse 14: What type of storm did Paul face? _____

Verse 17: When the boat was reeling in the waves and about to be broken up by the fierce storm, what did they do to reinforce and strengthen the ship?

_____

≈**Nugget**≈   The King James Bible tells us they used "helps" to undergird the ship. These helps were giant ropes which were on board. The sailers wrapped and undergirded the ship with giant ropes to help strengthen the boat and to keep it from falling apart in the storm. These ropes helped keep the ship together in a time of stress! In the same way, God's grace helps us in the midst of storms, stress and pressure. He wraps us up in His grace ropes and strengthens us to withstand the beating that the pace of life sometimes gives us.

3.	Zechariah 4:7

Underline the words we are to shout.

"Who are you, O great mountain? Before Zerubbabel you shall become a plain! And he shall bring forth the capstone with shouts of "Grace, grace to it!" NKJV

What did they cry out against the obstacles and mountains that stood in their way?

_____

Have you shouted "grace" to the mountains of stress and obstacles of overload in your life by faith?

_____

God offers you real, tangible grace to help you in your time of need. When you're feeling overwhelmed, overloaded and overstressed, there is grace to help! Start shouting!

God Gives You People To Help

1.	Exodus 18:13-26

In this lengthy passage, underline verses 14, 18, 21 and 23.

13 The next day Moses took his seat to serve as judge for the people, and they stood around him from morning till evening. 14 When his father-in-law saw all that Moses was doing for the people, he said, "What is this you are doing for the people? Why do you alone sit as judge, while all these people stand around you from morning till evening?" 15 Moses answered him, "Because the people come to me to seek God's will. 16 Whenever they have a dispute, it is brought to me, and I decide between the parties and inform them of God's decrees and laws." 17 Moses' father-in-law replied, "What you are doing is not good. 18 You and these people who come to you will only wear yourselves out. The work is too heavy for you; you cannot handle it alone. 19 Listen now to me and I will give you some advice, and may God be with you. You must be the people's representative before God and bring their disputes to him. 20 Teach them the decrees and laws, and show them the way to live and the duties they are to perform. 21 But select capable men from all the people — men who fear God, trustworthy men who hate dishonest gain — and appoint them as officials over thousands, hundreds, fifties and tens. 22 Have them serve as judges for the people at all times, but have them bring every difficult case to you; the simple cases they can decide themselves. That will make your load lighter, because they will share it with you. 23 If you do this and God so commands, you will be able to stand the strain, and all these people will go home satisfied." 24 Moses listened to his father-in-law and did everything he said. 25 He chose capable men from all Israel and made them leaders of the people, officials over thousands, hundreds, fifties and tens. 26 They served as judges for the people at all times. The difficult cases they brought to Moses, but the simple ones they decided themselves. NIV

It's a reality that you and I cannot do it all alone! We need help. Moses faced this overload challenge and was finally given godly counsel from his father-in-law.

What was Moses trying to do by himself?

_____

What did Moses' father-in-law tell him about this unhealthy practice?

_____

Do all the good you can, in all the ways you can, to all the souls you can, in every place you can, with all the zeal you can, as long as you ever can.

John Wesley

What does verse 17 tell us about doing this alone? _____

Trying to do it all by yourself is too heavy. It's not God's plan. We need help. Do you believe that God will connect you to people that will be a help to you and those that you can help?

What did God's counsel look like? _____

In the end, what kind of people did God use to help Moses?

_____

What does verse 23 promise us if we get help?

_____

2.   Numbers 11:11-17

Underline verses 14 and 17.

"11 And Moses said to the LORD, "Why are you treating me, your servant, so miserably? What did I do to deserve the burden of a people like this? 12 Are they my children? Am I their father? Is that why you have told me to carry them in my arms — like a nurse carries a baby — to the land you swore to give their ancestors? 13 Where am I supposed to get meat for all these people? They keep complaining and saying, 'Give us meat!' 14 I can't carry all these people by myself! The load is far too heavy! 15 I'd rather you killed me than treat me like this. Please spare me this misery!" 16 Then the LORD said to Moses, "Summon before me seventy of the leaders of Israel. Bring them to the Tabernacle to stand there with you. 17 I will come down and talk to you there. I will take some of the Spirit that is upon you, and I will put the Spirit upon them also. They will bear the burden of the people along with you, so you will not have to carry it alone." NLT

Moses was feeling the heavy load of leading the people of Israel and realized that he could not do it alone.

What did Moses tell the Lord in verse 14? _____

What did Moses ask the Lord for? _____

What was the Lord's response? _____

We need godly relief to overcome overloaded lives. If you sometimes feel that the load you carry is too much for you, begin to believe God for divine connections and the right people to come into your life to help you in whatever area you require help.

God Gives You Wisdom And Peace To Help

1.   Psalm 29:11

Underline the phrases "God makes" and "God gives."

GOD makes his people strong. GOD gives his people peace.
The Message

What does God make? _____

What does God give? _____

2.   Proverbs 3:13-18

Underline the words "wisdom" and "understanding."

13 Happy is the man who finds wisdom, and the man who gains understanding; 14 For her proceeds are better than the profits of silver, and her gain than fine gold. 15 She is more precious than rubies, and all the things you may desire cannot compare with her. 16 Length of days is in her right hand, in her left hand riches and honor. 17 Her ways are ways of pleasantness, and all her paths are peace. 18 She is a tree of life to those who take hold of her, and happy are all who retain her. NKJV

List all the things God promises to us when we walk in wisdom and understanding:

_____

_____

_____

_____

3.   John 14:27, 16:33

Underline the word "peace."

14:27 Peace I leave with you, My peace I give to you; not as the world gives do I give to you. Let not your heart be troubled, neither let it be afraid. NKJV

16:33 These things I have spoken to you, that in Me you may have peace. In the world you will have tribulation; but be of good cheer, I have overcome the world. NKJV

What did Jesus promise us? _____

Scriptures To Chew On

Taking time to meditate on and memorize God's Word is invaluable. Hiding His Word in our hearts will strengthen us for the present and arm us for the future. Here are two verses to memorize and chew on this week. Write these verses on index cards and carry them with you this week. If you will post them in your bathroom, dashboard, desk, locker or other convenient places, you will find these Scriptures taking root in your heart.

> *"So do not fear, for I am with you;*
> *do not be dismayed, for I am your God.*
> *I will strengthen you and help you;*
> *I will uphold you and with my righteous right hand."*
> *Isaiah 41:10, NIV*

> *"God is our refuge and strength,*
> *A very present help in trouble."*
> *Psalm 46:1, NKJV*

Group Discussion

1. Describe a time you tried to do a job alone. How was it? Have you considered seeking or hiring help?

2. Describe the way God's grace helps to strengthen you.

3. Describe an area in your life where you need more grace to help.

Personal Notes

How Do You Spell Relief?

Session Three

Anyone that can run 26 miles impresses me! A few years ago my husband Jeff, along with 35,000 others, ran the Chicago Marathon. I was so proud of him. One thing the runners did was pace themselves. When the gun goes off everyone starts with a rush of adrenaline and energy, but they realize that they cannot keep a starting pace for the entire 26 miles, so they look for their stride that will allow them to finish the race. As my husband expended more and more energy during the race, he needed replenishment. He needed glucose and water to continually energize and hydrate his body so that he wouldn't wear out before the finish line. It would have been crazy for him to presume to run the race at his pace without some type of relief along the way. In the same way, we need God's grace to help us keep the pace and finish our race!

As we stood in the grandstands that day watching everyone cross the finish line of the Chicago Marathon, I had a God moment. I thought, *"Lord, this is what You see everyday. People finish their race on Earth and they cross that heavenly finish line."* Some of those in the Chicago Marathon finished the race strong, energized and full of joy. Many people finished with a limp or a stagger and others crawled across the finish line. God wants all of us to finish our race of faith with joy. We need His grace for the pace to keep us strengthened and replenished for an entire lifetime. His grace brings us the relief we need in our race.

We Need To Be Replenished

Bill Hybels, Senior Pastor of Willowcreek Church, has a great illustration about the three gauges each one of us lives by. He talks about the need to replenish your

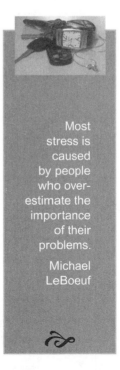

> Most stress is caused by people who over-estimate the importance of their problems.
>
> Michael LeBoeuf

emotional, spiritual and physical tanks. We cannot run on empty. It's important to be recharged and to refuel.

Psalm 23:3

Underline the part of you God promises to restore.

. . . he restores my soul. He guides me in paths of righteousness for his name's sake. NIV

What does God promise to do for our soul? _____

Our soul includes our mind, emotions and will. Not only do we need spiritual and physical restoration, we need it in our soul. Let's look at some of the ways He restores, refreshes, replenishes and refuels us.

Upload Your Cares

Imagine a marathon runner trying to race wearing a ski jacket, hiking boots and motorcycle helmet. It would be too big of a burden, and just the weight of the extra clothing would wear the runner out! Often in life, we are like that runner. As we run our race, we carry the weight of the world, worries, cares and burdens which weigh us down. We need to unload. We need to cast our cares and get some relief. We need to upload our concerns to the Lord.

1.   Hebrews 12:1

        Underline all the things we are to throw off.

        Therefore, since we are surrounded by such a great cloud of witnesses, let us throw off everything that hinders and the sin that so easily entangles, and let us run with perseverance the race marked out for us. NIV

        God has a race for you to run and finish!

        How are we to run? _____

What sins and weights could you discard as you keep pace in your race?

_____

Who do we keep our eyes on in this race? _____

2.   Psalm 55:22

Underline the phrase "cast your cares on the Lord."

Cast your cares on the LORD and he will sustain you; he will never let the righteous fall. NIV

Cares are heavy!

What does God tell us to do with our cares? _____

What worries do you need to hand over to the Lord once and for all?

_____

What does God promise you? _____

3.   Matthew 11:28-30

Underline verse 30.

28 Are you tired? Worn out? Burned out on religion? Come to me. Get away with me and you'll recover your life. I'll show you how to take a real rest. 29 Walk with me and work with me — watch how I do it. Learn the unforced rhythms of grace. I won't lay anything heavy or ill-fitting on you. 30 Keep company with me and you'll learn to live freely and lightly. The Message

If you are tired, worn out, burned out and overloaded, who should you run to first?

_____

What does Jesus want us to do? _____

What does Jesus promise you? _____

In what way is this passage relevant for you? _____

Know Your Limitations

Sometimes we are our own worst enemy. We don't know how to set boundaries. We don't say no. We create our own stress by not recognizing our God-given limitations.

&**Nugget**&   It might be good to ask yourself some basic questions. What has God called and gifted you to do? What season of life are you in? Have you recognized the importance of blending your calling and gifts with the season of life you are in? How many plates has God called you to spin? Often, we are stressed in the pace of life because we are putting more pressure on ourselves than God Himself puts on us! Maybe you are the type of person that has a hard time saying no. Maybe you are doing many things that you aren't even called or graced to do. Maybe you are financially overextended in an attempt to keep up with the Joneses. Often we live beyond our limitations. Real faith recognizes God-ordained boundaries, which are where God's giftings, graces and callings start and stop.

1.   2 Corinthians 10:13-16

        Underline the phrase "the field God has assigned to us."

        *13 We, however, will not boast beyond proper limits, but will confine
        our boasting to the field God has assigned to us, a field that reaches
        even to you. 14 We are not going too far in our boasting, as would be*

the case if we had not come to you, for we did get as far as you with the gospel of Christ. 15 Neither do we go beyond our limits by boasting of work done by others. Our hope is that, as your faith continues to grow, our area of activity among you will greatly expand, 16 so that we can preach the gospel in the regions beyond you. For we do not want to boast about work already done in another man's territory. NIV

In this passage, the Holy Spirit, through the Apostle Paul, explains the importance of knowing your limitations. When we try to do more than God has called us to do, we run the risk of falling into pride which will lead to overload and burnout. Sure, there may be some people that fit in the "superman" or "superwoman" category that seemingly "do it all," but what has God called you to focus on?

Sometimes we face unnecessary stress and a sense of overload because we are being disobedient in doing more than God desires.

Where did Paul say he would spend his ministry efforts?

_____

He determined not to presume authority, rights or gifts that would infringe upon another person's accomplishments or sphere of ministry.

How is this passage relevant in your life and staying within your sphere and limitations?

_____

_____

&**Nugget**& If you are used to operating in God's grace, then it is usually easy to discern when you are operating outside of God's grace. The symptoms of operating outside of God's

What
gets
rewarded,
gets
done.

Unknown

grace commonly include: unusual frustration, dissatisfaction, things just not working, physical symptoms in our bodies, emotional unrest, and as someone once put it, *"it feels like taking a shower with your socks on!"* Things just don't flow. Everything seems difficult. Does this describe any facet of your life?

2.   John 5:30

Underline the phrases that describe Jesus' submission to God's will.

I am able to do nothing from Myself [independently, of My own accord—but only as I am taught by God and as I get His orders]. Even as I hear, I judge [I decide as I am bidden to decide. As the voice comes to Me, so I give a decision], and My judgment is right (just, righteous), because I do not seek or consult My own will [I have no desire to do what is pleasing to Myself, My own aim, My own purpose] but only the will and pleasure of the Father Who sent Me. AMP

Jesus, the Master, knew how to stay submitted to God's will.

Where did Jesus get His orders? _____

What was Jesus' focus with His time and energy? _____

Did Jesus "self-generate" His life and consult His own will?

_____

Who did Jesus want to please? _____

This is the recipe for a stress-free life.

3.   1 Peter 4:10, Romans 12:6

Underline the words "gifts" or "grace."

As each of you has received a gift (a particular spiritual talent, a gracious divine endowment), employ it for one another as [befits] good trustees of God's many-sided grace [faithful stewards of the extremely diverse powers and gifts granted to Christians by unmerited favor].
1 Peter 4:10, AMP

Having gifts (faculties, talents, qualities) that differ according to the grace given us, let us use them... Romans 12:6, AMP

In these passages, we are encouraged to use the gifts God has given us. These "grace" gifts are free gifts and abilities the Lord has endowed us with. Living life and serving others is a joy when we are operating within our gifting.

What are we to do with our gifts? _____

Have you identified your God-given gifts?_____

Cultivate Your God-Given Friendships

As many friendship experts have said, the relationships in our life either drain us or replenish us. There are high maintenance friends and there are those that pour blessing and refreshment into our lives. Be sure to cultivate the friendships God has given you; they are a gift for refreshing your life.

1.   Romans 15:32

        Underline the phrase "be refreshed" and "in your company."

        So that by God's will I may subsequently come to you with joy (with a happy heart) and be refreshed [by the interval of rest] in your company. AMP

        What did Paul say would happen for him and his friends when, by God's will, they were united?

_____

2.   1 Corinthians 16:17-18

Underline the phrase "they've refreshed me."

*17 I want you to know how delighted I am to have Stephanas,
Fortunatus, and Achaicus here with me. They partially make up for
your absence! 18 They've refreshed me by keeping me in touch with
you. Be proud that you have people like this among you. The Message*

Getting together with godly friends does what for your spirit?

_____

3.   2 Timothy 1:16-18

Underline the words that describe the blessing Onesiphorus was to Paul.

*16 The Lord grant mercy to the household of Onesiphorus, for he often
refreshed me, and was not ashamed of my chain; 17 but when he
arrived in Rome, he sought me out very zealously and found me. 18
The Lord grant to him that he may find mercy from the Lord in that
Day — and you know very well how many ways he ministered to me
at Ephesus. NKJV*

Friends who share your love for Christ provide what? _____

4.   Philemon 7

Underline the phrase "great joy and encouragement" and "refreshed."

*Your love has given me great joy and encouragement, because you,
brother, have refreshed the hearts of the saints. NIV*

God's love through our friends does what for us? _____

One of God's greatest blessings are people! Sometimes just talking or praying with a friend does wonders for our stress level. Be sure to appreciate and cultivate the friendships God has placed in your life and you will find relief from much of the stress and overload in your life.

Scriptures To Chew On

Taking time to meditate on and memorize God's Word is invaluable. Hiding His Word in our hearts will strengthen us for the present and arm us for the future. Here are two verses to memorize and chew on this week. Write these verses on index cards and carry them with you this week. If you will post them in your bathroom, dashboard, desk, locker or other convenient places, you will find these Scriptures taking root in your heart.

"I can do all things through Christ who strengthens me."
Philippians 4:13, NKJV

"Cast your cares on the LORD and he will sustain you;
he will never let the righteous fall."
Psalm 55:22, NIV

Group Discussion

1. Describe the way you cast your cares on the Lord. Is this something you do on a regular basis or do you tend to hold your cares and worry?

2. Describe the season you are in; the assignments you know God has given to you and the limitations you must keep.

3. Describe the replenishing friendships God has given you. Who's your "go to" friend in times of crisis, need and rejoicing? In life some relationships are "draining" and some are "replenishing." Do you have more replenishing relationships than draining ones?

Personal Notes

Personal Notes

56

Personal Notes

Get A Bigger Frying Pan

How would you like to run to a tropical island all by yourself, lay in the sun under the beautiful palm trees, read your favorite books and sip fresh-squeezed lemonade? Wanna run away from stress and overload? Sorry, it's time to snap back to reality. For most of us, this unfortunately isn't an option.

Stress and overloaded lives are a reality. Is there anything we can do to eliminate the pressures and pace we face? At times, we can and should cut back and cut out things to reduce the pace of life. At other times, we need to receive more "grace to help" in order to overcome. Still at other times, we just need a dose of relief and replenishment to carry us along.

The reality is that often we can't do anything to eliminate, limit or retreat from our "overloaded-ness." What do you do then? What if stress and life's pace "is what it is," and we just have to deal with it? Then what?

Good news: there is a solution! If we cannot limit the amount of stress being poured into our lives, then we need to enlarge our capacity for dealing with overload.

It's like the story about grandma's ham. One day Helen Housewife was preparing dinner as little Suzie looked on. Suzie watched her mother cut both ends off the ham before she placed it in the frying pan. Suzie asked her mother why she cut the ends off, and Helen Housewife said it was because her mother and her grandmother did it that way. One day Suzie asked her grandmother why she cuts both ends of the ham off before placing it in the frying pan. Grandmother responded, "That's easy, it's

Future Shock is the shattering stress and disorientation that we induce in individuals by subjecting them to too much change in too short a time.

Alvin Toffler

the only way the ham would fit in my frying pan." Grandma and Helen Housewife really didn't need to cut the ends of the ham off; they just needed a bigger frying pan! Often, we are doing things the way others do them, only to find out there is a better way. God has bigger frying pans, and in this chapter we will discover how to obtain them!

Have you ever tried to blow up a fresh balloon? The smallest ones are the hardest. It takes effort and a lot of air pressure to fill that balloon for the first time. Once it's inflated and you let the air out, have you noticed that it's quite a bit easier the second time you blow it up? The capacity for air was increased the first time it was blown up. Blowing it up the first time was the hardest, but the air pressure inside the balloon actually stretched it and enlarged its capacity for future uses. It's the same with our lives. God wants to help us enlarge the balloon of our ability to keep pace by enlarging our capacity to handle stress and overload. When God begins to enlarge our capacity, often it's tough at first and we feel the pressure. It feels like we'll burst, but usually the Lord allows just enough pressure to enlarge our capacity.

Later, when we face other pressures, responsibilities and the increased pace of life, it's amazing how easily our enlarged capacity is able to cope and overcome. It seems that each season of life brings increasing demands. When we are students, young adults or single, there is a certain pace we must keep. As we enter the work force and take on more responsibility the pace seems to increase. If we marry and begin a family, the pace picks up again. Many variables factor in over the course of our lives and play a role in determining the stress and overload level we face. For each season the pace increases, we will likely find God enlarging our capacity and resources to effectively handle the pressures of life.

Richard Swenson, author of the excellent book *Margin: Restoring Emotional, Physical, Financial, and Time Reserves to Overloaded Lives* says, *"Overload is not having time to finish the book you're reading on stress. Margin is having time to read it twice. Overload is fatigue. Margin is energy. Overload is red ink. Margin is black ink. Overload is hurry. Margin is calm. Overload is anxiety. Margin is security. Overload is the disease of the '90s. Margin is the cure."* [1]

His book says, *"As a medical practitioner, Dr. Richard Swenson sees a steady stream of exhausted, hurting people coming into his office. A majority of them are suffering from an uncontrolled societal epidemic: living without margin. Margin is the space that once existed between ourselves and our limits. It's something held in reserve for contingencies or unanticipated situations. As a society, we've forgotten what margin is. In the push for progress, margin has been devoured. So we feel distressed in ill-defined ways. We are besieged by anxiety, stress, and fatigue. Our relationships suffer. We have unexplained aches and pains. The flood of daily events seems beyond our control. We're overloaded. If you yearn for relief from the pain and pressure of overload, take a lifelong dose of Margin under the care of a specialist. The benefits of good health, financial stability, fulfilling relationships, and availability for God's purposes will follow you all your days."*

In his book, Dr. Swenson provides a prescription against the danger of overloaded lives. Focusing on margin in four key areas—emotional energy, physical energy, time and finances. He shows us how contentment, simplicity, balance and rest provide us with a healthy lifestyle.

"Margin" is an excellent book and I highly recommend it. In this study we'll see the Bible refers to this concept of margin as "enlarged capacity."

&**Nugget**& In the first chapter of Dr. Swenson's book, he describes the scenario of taking a glass of water and adding salt by the teaspoonful. When the salt is stirred into the water it dissolves. If salt is continually added to the water, eventually the salt will not dissolve. The water is salt saturated and the margin for dissolving salt is over. The only solution is to quit adding salt or to enlarge the cup and then add more water.

In our lives, often we cannot stop the salt from coming into our glasses of water, but we can enlarge our container! Let's look at this.

1.   Psalm 4:1

        Underline the word "enlarged."

ANSWER ME when I call, O God of my righteousness (uprightness, justice, and right standing with You)! You have freed me when I was hemmed in and enlarged me when I was in distress; have mercy upon me and hear my prayer. AMP

When we are in distress and call out to the Lord in prayer, what will He do for us?

_____

Enlarge: This means to broaden and is sometimes translated as enlarged, make large, make room, make open wide.[2]

When God enlarges, makes large, makes room and makes open wide our hearts, we have the capacity to handle more!

2.   Samuel 22:37

Underline the word "enlarged."

You enlarged my path under me; so my feet did not slip. NKJV

What will God do to the path we are on?_____

What does enlarging our path help us with? _____

3.   1 Chronicles 4:10

Underline the word "enlarge."

And Jabez called on the God of Israel saying, "Oh, that You would bless me indeed, and enlarge my territory, that Your hand would be with me, and that You would keep me from evil, that I may not cause pain!" So God granted him what he requested. NKJV

We know the story of Jabez and his prayer. In order to have the influence God had called him to function in, what four things did Jabez need?

_____ _____

_____ _____

What was God's response to Jabez? _____

4. Isaiah 54:2-3

Underline the word "enlarge."

2 Enlarge the place of your tent, and let them stretch out the curtains of your dwellings; do not spare; lengthen your cords, and strengthen your stakes. 3 For you shall expand to the right and to the left, and your descendants will inherit the nations, and make the desolate cities inhabited. NKJV

God knows all about your life and future. He helps us to prepare for the pace and load we carry.

What did He tell the Israelites to do prior to their increase and growth?

_____

_____

5. Psalm 138:3

Underline the word "large."

The moment I called out, you stepped in; you made my life large with strength. The Message

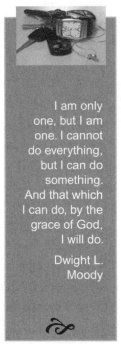

I am only one, but I am one. I cannot do everything, but I can do something. And that which I can do, by the grace of God, I will do.

Dwight L. Moody

The minute we call out to God, He steps in and does what?

_____

6.   Isaiah 40:31

Underline the phrase "renew their strength."

But those who wait on the LORD shall renew their strength; they shall mount up with wings like eagles, they shall run and not be weary, they shall walk and not faint. NKJV

What does God promise to those who wait on the Lord?

_____

God is willing to give us new strength and enlarge our capacity as we call and wait upon Him.

God enlarges us with strength, wisdom, knowledge, strategies, energy, ideas, innovation, rest, ability, help and whatever we need. Isn't it wonderful to know God and trust Him to enlarge our capacity for each season?

Scriptures To Chew On

Taking time to meditate on and memorize God's Word is invaluable. Hiding His Word in our hearts will strengthen us for the present and arm us for the future. Here are two verses to memorize and chew on this week. Write these verses on index cards and carry them with you this week. If you will post them in your bathroom, dashboard, desk, locker or other convenient places, you will find these Scriptures taking root in your heart.

"But those who wait on the LORD shall renew their strength;
they shall mount up with wings like eagles,
they shall run and not be weary, they shall walk and not faint."
Isaiah 40:31, NKJV

"Enlarge the place of your tent,
and let them stretch out the curtains of your dwellings;
do not spare; lengthen your cords, and strengthen your stakes.
For you shall expand to the right and to the left . . ."
Isaiah 54:3-4, NKJV

Group Discussion

1.   Describe the margin in your life. Do you have any extra margin in any area of your life? Time? Energy? Finances? Mentally? Emotionally?

2.   Describe the areas where you need God to enlarge your capacity.

3.   Describe the power of waiting on the Lord and how He enlarges and strengthens you.

---

[1] Swenson, Richard. Margin: Restoring Emotional, Physical, Financial, and Time Resources to Overloaded Lives. Colorado Springs: NavPress, 1995

[2] Biblesoft's New Exhaustive Strong's Numbers and Concordance with Expanded Greek-Hebrew Dictionary. Copyright © 1994, 2003 Biblesoft, Inc. and International Bible Translators, Inc.

Personal Notes

A re you frustrating or accessing God's grace? It's great to know that God's grace is there to help us, but unfortunately many Christians are not tapping into it. They are not accessing God's grace, they are frustrating it! That's a problem, so let's take a look at this subject.

Accessing or Frustrating?

1. Galatians 2:21

    Underline the words "invalidate," "frustrate" and "nullify."

    [Therefore, I do not treat God's gracious gift as something of minor importance and defeat its very purpose]; I do not set aside and invalidate and frustrate and nullify the grace (unmerited favor) of God. AMP

    How should we esteem the grace of God?

    _____

    God's grace has a purpose and we want to be sure to tap into God's grace and experience its fullest effect in our lives.

    Is it possible to nullify or frustrate the grace?

    _____

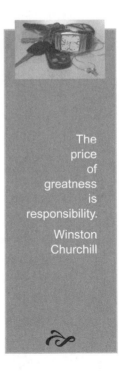

The price of greatness is responsibility.

Winston Churchill

How do you think we nullify or frustrate God's grace? _____

_____

When we do not esteem, focus on, validate and receive God's grace, we nullify and frustrate its ability to help us!

If you want to avoid frustrating or nullifying God's grace in your life, a good place to start is to simply make this prayerful acknowledgment: *"Father, I believe You have provided "grace to help" me in everything I face. I need your "grace for the pace" I am required to live and I don't want to frustrate or nullify it. I esteem Your grace and I ask You to help me to understand and access Your grace by faith. In Jesus' Name. Amen."*

2.   Romans 5:1-2

Underline the word "access by faith into this grace."

1 Therefore, since we have been justified through faith, we have peace with God through our Lord Jesus Christ, 2 through whom we have gained access by faith into this grace in which we now stand . . . NIV

What do we have access to through Christ? _____

What type of grace are we able to access? _____

How do we access the grace?_____

We receive and access God's grace simply by faith! You can't earn it. You can't work for it. You simply access God's grace by faith; that is what you believe in your heart and speak with your mouth. Start believing and speaking God's grace over your life. Access—don't frustrate—the grace for the pace!

What type of grace can we access by faith? Let's look at it.

Access God's Grace To Rule in Life

Romans 5:17

Underline the two things required for reigning in life.

. . . how much more will those who receive God's abundant provision of grace and of the gift of righteousness reign in life through the one man, Jesus Christ. NIV

What must you receive an abundance of in order to reign in life? _____

It is God's will that we live in victory. In the face of a busy pace and stress-filled times, God wants us to receive an abundance of His free gift of grace—His supernatural ability—so that we can rule in life as kings over anything contrary to His will.

Access God's Grace To Live Life

1 Peter 3:7

Underline the words "grace of life."

"Husbands, likewise, dwell with them with understanding, giving honor to the wife, as to the weaker vessel, and as being heirs together of the grace of life, that your prayers may not be hindered." NKJV

Husbands and wives are encouraged to live together in harmony in order to have an effective prayer life. Husbands and wives are to be heirs of what?

_____

How would you describe the "grace of life"? _____

What would your life look like if you were walking in the "grace of life"? _____

_____

Access God's Grace To Strengthen You

2 Corinthians 12:9-10

Underline the results of grace in this passage.

But He said to me, My grace (My favor and loving-kindness and mercy) is enough for you [sufficient against any danger and enables you to bear the trouble manfully]; for My strength and power are made perfect (fulfilled and completed) and show themselves most effective in [your] weakness. Therefore, I will all the more gladly glory in my weaknesses and infirmities, that the strength and power of Christ (the Messiah) may rest (yes, may pitch a tent over and dwell) upon me! So for the sake of Christ, I am well pleased and take pleasure in infirmities, insults, hardships, persecutions, perplexities and distresses; for when I am weak [in human strength], then am I [truly] strong (able, powerful in divine strength). AMP

Is God's grace enough for us? _____

What does grace enable us to do? _____

What does grace give us? _____

Through His grace, God gives us internal, divine strength to stand. When we are weak because of stressors, pressures, persecutions and a fast pace, then through His grace we can be strong.

Access God's Grace For Everything You Need

2 Corinthians 9:8

Underline the phrase "all grace."

"And God is able to make all grace (every favor and earthly blessing) come to you in abundance, so that you may always and under all circumstances and whatever the need be self-sufficient [possessing enough to require no aid or support and furnished in abundance for every good work and charitable donation]." AMP

What does God's grace give us? _____

Isn't this encouraging? These things are just the tip of the iceberg concerning the incredible, supernatural help God's grace imparts to us! I encourage you to do your own study in the Word to discover more benefits of God's grace.

Pray For Grace

Hebrews 4:16

Underline the phrases "come boldly" and "find grace."

Let us therefore come boldly to the throne of grace, that we may obtain mercy and find grace to help in time of need. NKJV

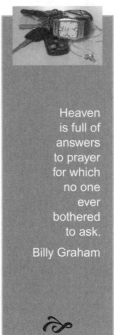

God promises to give you grace to help you. The way we access His grace is by coming boldly to His throne of grace.

Why can you come boldly to God's throne? _____

_____

What does God promise that you can obtain and find?

_____

Grace in all its forms can be accessed as you go boldly to God's throne in prayer!

Heaven is full of answers to prayer for which no one ever bothered to ask.

Billy Graham

Once more, let's pray for grace. *"Father, we are so thankful that because of the blood of Jesus Christ and our union with Him, we can come into Your Presence with boldness. You said I could obtain mercy and find grace to help at Your throne of grace and Father, I thank You for that. Right now, I appropriate your mercy and grace and I ask You to impart a fresh dose of grace into my life to help me in every arena. I thank You Lord that right now, I believe I receive a deposit of grace from Your very throne. Thank You. In Jesus' Name. Amen."*

Scriptures To Chew On

Taking time to meditate on and memorize God's Word is invaluable. Hiding His Word in our hearts will strengthen us for the present and arm us for the future. Here are two verses to memorize and chew on this week. Write these verses on index cards and carry them with you this week. If you will post them in your bathroom, dashboard, desk, locker or other convenient places, you will find these Scriptures taking root in your heart.

"For the LORD God is a sun and shield;
The LORD will give grace and glory;
No good thing will He withhold
From those who walk uprightly."
Psalm 84:11, NKJV

". . . how much more will those who receive
God's abundant provision of grace
and of the gift of righteousness
reign in life through the one man, Jesus Christ."
Romans 5:17b, NIV

Group Discussion

1.   Describe a time when you frustrated God's grace either through ignorance or not esteeming it.

2. Describe the way you will begin to access God's grace on a more regular basis.

3. Describe some of the specific applications of God's grace you'd like to access more.

Personal Notes

Time Keeps On Ticking

God's grace is available to help you manage and organize your time. Time management—or more importantly, life management—is an important part of overcoming stress and overload. Many things clutter our lives—schedules, deadlines, commitments, "shoulda, coulda, woulda" thoughts, sin and guilt, a messy home, desk or car, purposeless living—you name it. God wants to help us live an uncluttered life spirit, soul and body. Let's take a look at the subject of maximizing our lifetime.

Live On Purpose

People waste a lot of time and energy because they lack purpose. Without a purpose it's easy to become apathetic. The writer of Proverbs said, *"He also that is slothful in his work is brother to him that is a great waster." Proverbs 18:9, KJV* When we are lazy and slothful the pace of life will overtake us. It's important that we live on purpose and fulfill the reason we are alive and on Planet Earth. Let's talk about it.

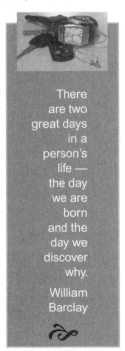

Ecclesiastes 3:11

Underline the phrase "a divinely implanted sense of a purpose."

He has made everything beautiful in its time. He also has planted eternity in men's hearts and minds [a divinely implanted sense of a purpose working through the ages which nothing under the sun but God alone can satisfy], yet so that men cannot find out what God has done from the beginning to the end. AMP

There are two great days in a person's life — the day we are born and the day we discover why.

William Barclay

ॐ

What does this tell us about our purpose? _____

_____

God has a divinely implanted sense of purpose for you! Isn't that a wonderful thought? You were born for a reason. You are not an accident. God planned for your arrival, whether your parents did or not. He has a divine purpose and plan for you and it's not His plan or purpose to burn you out with stress, pressure and overload.

Have you prayerfully sought the Lord to better identify His purpose for your life or season?

_____

What do you sense God's purpose for your life to be? _____

_____

_____

∾**Nugget**∾   Did you know that God's plan for your life is a blessed plan. Often, people have their own ideas and life plans and they ask God to slap His blessing on their plans. That's the backwards way to approach life. Why not seek the Lord on His plan and purpose for your life, knowing that His plan is already blessed? Many people live and die and never once step into their purpose for being alive. What a tragedy. God's plan and purpose for you will be revealed to your heart as you spend time reading His Word, praying and seeking Him. He's not hiding it from you. Make it your aim to spend some time laying your heart out before the Lord. Seek Him and His Word to discover your divinely implanted sense of purpose.

Discipline Yourself

1.   1 Corinthians 9:24-27

Underline the phrase "run in such a way as to get the prize."

24 Do you not know that in a race all the runners run, but only one gets the prize? Run in such a way as to get the prize. 25 Everyone who competes in the games goes into strict training. They do it to get a crown that will not last; but we do it to get a crown that will last forever. 26 Therefore I do not run like a man running aimlessly; I do not fight like a man beating the air. 27 No, I beat my body and make it my slave so that after I have preached to others, I myself will not be disqualified for the prize. NIV

As we move through life, it's good to know where the finish line is. What goals are you reaching for?

_____

In what ways could you or should you discipline your life to win the race, specifically in these areas: personal Bible study, prayer, exercise, diet, giving, time management, mentally, etc?

_____

_____

What type of crown are we running for? _____

What did the Apostle Paul say he did to himself in order to win and not be disqualified.

_____

Nugget If we want to live a stress-free life, we will have to discipline ourselves. We'll have to make our minds, bodies, emotions submit to our spirit. Health professionals will tell you about the importance of diet and exercise when it comes to releasing the stress in your life. When it comes to managing our time, relationships, diet, exercise, sleep, time with God, spiritual growth and mental development, it takes discipline. The pay off is huge—intimacy with God, strength and health in our bodies, peace of mind and favor with God and man—it's worth every bit of determination it takes to live a disciplined life.

It goes without saying that if we live the life of the workaholic, alcoholic and foodaholic, we are bound to be stressed and overloaded. If we smoke, party and binge, it's likely that our lives will not be what God intended. Let's run, fight the good fight and keep the faith as we finish the race that is set before us. Let's finish our course with joy!

2.   1 Timothy 4:8-9

Underline the phrases "workouts in the gymnasium" and "disciplined life."

Workouts in the gymnasium are useful, but a disciplined life in God is far more so, making you fit both today and forever. 9 You can count on this. Take it to heart. The Message

When it comes to reducing stress in our lives, fitness training, workouts, diet and rest play an important role. Although we have not focused on this in our study, it is important to consider the fuel and exercise you are giving your body and the affect this has on stress hormones in your body.

As useful as exercise is, what is even more valuable? _____

_____

Have An Organized Plan

Living a disorganized, unstructured, fly-by-the-seat-of-the-pants life will only add stress and pressure to an overloaded life. It's true that when we take the time to organize our lives—our work, our homes and our personal lives—we will actually bring a sense of calm, peace and order to our lives.

1.   Proverbs 24:3

Underline the words "wise planning," "common sense" and "keeping abreast of the facts."

Any enterprise is built by wise planning, becomes strong through common sense, and profits wonderfully by keeping abreast of the facts. TLB

If we want a healthy life, what three things should we pay attention to?

_____

_____

2.   1 Corinthians 14:40

Underline the words, "decently" and "order."

Let all things be done decently and in order. NKJV

How should we do things?

_____

People always make time to do the things they really want to do.

Anonymous

In what practical ways could you add order to your life and responsibilities?

⸘**Nugget**⸘ One of the best helps for being organized is to begin to think categorically and systematically. For example, I remember when my two boys were around the ages of 5 and 7, I asked them to clean their bedroom. Their room was a disaster. Socks, toys, sports gear, shoes and clothing were all over the place. I moved all the junk to the middle of the room and told them, *"Ok boys, clean your room and I'll check back in about twenty minutes."* They sat down and cried. I realized that this project was overwhelming to their little minds. Where would they begin? I knew that I needed to get them to think categorically and systematically, so I told them we'd take this project in little bites. First, I told them to just search for the socks and put them in a pile, then search for all the little cars and puzzle pieces, and eventually we'd whittle the big pile down by organizing things by category into little piles.

If the responsibilities, tasks and pace of your life sometimes seems like a big, disorganized, overwhelming pile, take a minute to think about how you could systematically and categorically restructure your life into little piles.

Have you noticed that often when your schedule is organized, your time is managed and clutter is organized, it clears your mind from stressed and overwhelming thoughts?

3. Habakkuk 2:2-3

Underline the phrase "Write the vision."

Then the LORD answered me and said: "Write the vision and make it plain on tablets, that he may run who reads it. 3 For the vision is yet for an appointed time; but at the end it will speak, and it will not lie. Though it tarries, wait for it; because it will surely come, it will not tarry. NKJV

What should we write down?_____

Do you have a vision or a plan for your life? Family? Career? Ministry? Do you have a plan for this year? This month? This week? Today? Write it down! Write your vision in such a practical way that when you read it you are motivated to run with it. Keep it simple. Strategic. Practical.

If you can articulate your vision on paper, it's very likely that this will become your personal roadmap. Often getting things off our minds and on paper has a way of relieving mental stress and disorganizational overload. Do yourself a favor and write down the things you envision for your life, your year, your month, your week and your day. Jot down any plans or strategies the Lord has given you for accomplishing those things.

Maximize Your Time

For every season there is a time!

1.   Psalm 90:12

        Underline the phrase "teach us to number our days."

        So teach us to number our days, that we may gain a heart of wisdom.
        NKJV

        God wants us to live life on and with purpose.

        How can you number your days? _____

        ≋**Nugget**≋   To calculate the ballpark number of your days just work this mathematical formula. Take the number of the age you expect and desire to live to be and subtract your current age from that number. The result will give you a basic number of your days. For example, let's say you are currently 35 years old and you expect to live to 95 years old. If you subtract 35 from 95 you get 60, right? That tells us that this person has around 60 years left.

What is your current age? _____

To what age do you desire, believe and expect to live? _____

What is the estimated number of your days? _____

2.   Psalm 31:15

Underline each word.

My times are in your hands... NIV

Who's hands are our times in?_____

3.   Jeremiah 2:8

Underline the phrase "wasted their time on nonsense."

Even their priests cared nothing for the Lord, and their judges ignored me; their rulers turned against me, and their prophets worshiped Baal and wasted their time on nonsense. TLB

This passage tells us that God's ministers were living in an ungodly way.

What can we learn about the use of our time?_____

_____

What would you consider "nonsense" to be? _____

4.   Ephesians 5:15-16

Underline the phrase "making the most."

15 Be very careful, then, how you live-not as unwise but as wise, 16 making the most of every opportunity, because the days are evil. NIV

How should we live? _____

_____

What does "make the most of every opportunity" mean to you? _____

_____

❧Nugget❧   Do you have a plan for managing your time? Whether you use a commercial planning system, computer program or you create your own, it's amazing how much more effective we can be with our time if we spend some time planning. Also, consider using your time twice! For example, you know you have to eat lunch each day, why not use your lunch hour to meet with people or to read faith-building or life-enhancing books? By using yearly view and monthly view calendars, checklists and daily planners, you will maximize your time and make the most of every opportunity. Structure your time so that you schedule your activities and tasks in blocks. For example, run all your errands at one time, make all your phone conversations during a specific block of time, etc. It's also wise to use your best time, when you're most alert, for the most important things. I encourage you to be proactive in taking back your time and maximizing every moment.

5.   Ecclesiastes 8:5-6

Underline the phrases "a wise man's mind will know" and "right time."

5 ...and a wise man's mind will know both when and what to do. 6 For every purpose and matter has its [right] time and judgment... AMP

What does a wise man know? _____

What does every purpose and matter have? _____

As you walk with God and in the light of His Word, He will fill you with wisdom and your wise mind will know both when and what to do! By God's grace you will live a life of peace and joy, free from stress and overload.

There is grace for the pace! As we learn to live on purpose, to live with an organized plan and to maximize our time, we will find that order brings a great sense of stability and freedom from stress to our lives.

Scriptures To Chew On

Taking time to meditate on and memorize God's Word is invaluable. Hiding His Word in our hearts will strengthen us for the present and arm us for the future. Here are two verses to memorize and chew on this week. Write these verses on index cards and carry them with you this week. If you will post them in your bathroom, dashboard, desk, locker or other convenient places, you will find these Scriptures taking root in your heart.

"To every thing there is a season,
and a time to every purpose under the heaven . . ."
Ecclesiastes 3:1, KJV

". . . a wise man's mind will know both when and what to do.
For every purpose and matter has its [right] time and judgment . . ."
Ecclesiastes 8:5-6, AMP

Group Discussion

1.   Describe what you understand about God's purpose for your life. Share any verses of Scripture the Lord has given you about your purpose.

2.   Describe the areas of your life that need more discipline, vision and planning.

3.   Describe your plan for managing your time and numbering your days.

Personal Notes

Personal Notes

Personal Notes

The "Bite Sized Bible Study Series"
By Beth Jones

*When your words came, I ate them;
they were my joy and my heart's delight . . .
Jeremiah 15:16 NIV*

- Six practical Bible studies for Christians living in today's culture.
- Each book contains 6 sessions designed for individual & small group study.
- Great studies targeting men, women, believers and seekers of all ages.
- Convenient size 6" x 9", each book is between 80-144 pages.
- Fill-in-the-blank book with Group Discussion questions after each session.
- "Nuggets" throughout each study explain Scriptures in easy to follow way.
- Written in a contemporary style using practical illustrations.
- Perfect for small group curriculum, bookstores and churches.

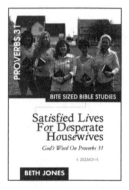

Satisfied Lives For Desperate Housewives
God's Word On Proverbs 31
Great Study For Women, Retail $7.99
ISBN: 1-933433-04-3

Session 1: Desperate For God
Session 2: Desperate For Balance
Session 3: Desperate For A Good Marriage
Session 4: Desperate For Godly Kids
Session 5: Desperate To Serve
Session 6: Desperate For Purpose

Grace For The Pace
God's Word For Stressed & Overloaded Lives
Great Study For Men & Women, Retail $7.99
ISBN: 1-933433-02-7

Session 1: Escape From Hamsterville
Session 2: Help Is Here
Session 3: How Do You Spell Relief?
Session 4: Get A Bigger Frying Pan
Session 5: Houston, We Have A Problem!
Session 6: Time Keeps On Ticking

Call Or Go Online To Order:
800-596-0379
www.valleypresspublishers.com

Kissed Or Dissed

God's Word For Rejection & Feeling Overlooked
Great Study For Women, Retail $7.99
ISBN: 1-933433-01-9

Session 1: Dissed 101
Session 2: Blessed & Highly Favored
Session 3: Edit Your Life
Session 4: That's What I'm Talking About
Session 5: Sow Acceptance Seeds
Session 6: Just Like Jesus

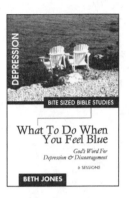

What To Do When You Feel Blue

God's Word For Depression & Discouragement
Great Study For Men & Women, Retail $7.99
ISBN: 1-933433-00-0

Session 1: When The Sky Is Not Blue
Session 2: No Pity Parties Allowed
Session 3: The Things You Could Think
Session 4: Go To Your Happy Place
Session 5: You've Got To Have Friends
Session 6: Lift Up The Down

The Friends God Sends

God's Word On Friendship & Chick Chat
Great Study For Women, Retail $7.99
ISBN: 1-933433-05-1

Session 1: Friendship Realities
Session 2: The Friendship Workout
Session 3: God-Knit Friendships
Session 4: Who's On Your Boat?
Session 5: Anatomy Of A Friendship Famine
Session 6: A Friend Of God

Don't Factor Fear Here

God's Word For Overcoming Anxiety, Fear & Phobias
Great Study For Men & Women, Retail $7.99
ISBN: 1-933433-03-5

Session 1: Fear of Death
Session 2: Fear of Man
Session 3: Fear of Danger
Session 4: Fear of Change
Session 5: Fear Factors - Peace & Love
Session 6: Fear Factors - Faith & Courage

Why The Gory, Bloody Details?
By Beth Jones

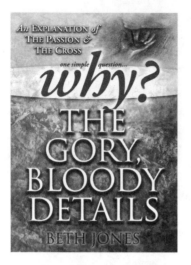

. . . right before
your very eyes--
Jesus Christ
(the Messiah)
was openly
and graphically
set forth
and
portrayed
as crucified . . .
Galatians 3:1, AMP

Why The Gory, Bloody Details?
An Explanation of the Passion and the Cross

Retail Paperback $4.99, Hardcover $7.99

ISBN: 0-9717156-6-1 Paperback
ISBN: 0-9717156-7-X Hardcover

This contagious 96-page giftbook answers the basic question, "Why did Jesus have to die on the cross?" People want to know: Why did Jesus endure such brutality? Why did God allow His own Son to be murdered? Why the gore and blood? It's a great evangelistic gift for unsaved friends and family and a great educational resource for believers who want to understand the cross and the passion.

- *Evangelistic gift book explains the cross—perfect for seekers.*
- *Gospel presented in a relevant, easy to understand way.*
- *Gift book size 4" x 6", 96 pages.*
- *Written in a contemporary style using practical illustrations.*
- *Hardcover and paperback.*

VALLEY PRESS
PUBLISHERS

A Ministry of Kalamazoo Valley Family Church
995 Romence Road
Portage, MI 49024
Ph. 800-596-0379
www.valleypresspublishers.com